Deluged with Dudes

Platonic & Erotic Love Poems to Men

by

alta

Shameless Hussy Press

Some of these poems and recollections have appeared in
Freedom's in Sight, No Visible Means of Support, Song of
the Wife/ Song of the Mistress, City Miners, Clock Radio,
Berkeley Poetry Review, No More Masks, I Am Not a Practicing
Angel, & Understanding Modern Poetry.

ISBN: 0 • 915288 • 59 • 1

Photograph of John Oliver Simon & alta by Brad Lehman

Photograph of alta by Harold Parrish

Book Design: William Henderson III

Shameless Hussy Press

Box 5540

Berkeley, California 94705

This book is dedicated to
my lawyer, Gerald, who saved my house,
Doctor H., who saved my life,
& my bro, Bill Art, who saves my ass on a
regular basis.

flourishing & withering are fated
stop coveting, stop plotting
simply approach the thing in the cup

> *Kuan Yün-Shih*
> *translated by Jerome P. Seaton*

in my dreams
I hold my lovers
next to me all at once
and ask them

what was it I desired?

my hands are full
of their heads
like bunches of cut roses
blond hair, brown hair, red, black
their eyes are pools of bewilderment
staring up at me
from the bouquet

what was it I desired?
I ask again...

did I think I could escape,
by taking your breath
into my mouth,
did I think I could escape
the responsibility
of breathing?

...what
I yell at them
shaking my lovers
what did I desire in you?

> Mary Mackey, *Desire*

PREFACE

As I sat alone at Giovanni's tonight, I realized there was nothing I'd rather do than come home & work on my book of love poems. But what an alternative to spending the night with a passionate lover!

In two weeks, I am leaving to visit a recent favorite in Atlanta, but I am pursuing him, he has not pursued me. After all the men who have followed me, I am now the one doing the following. Mom laughs, "Lo! How the mighty are fallen!"

I used to look forward to being older so that men wouldn't annoy me constantly, but would treat me as a whole human being. Instead, they went from treating me like a pussy with a person attached, to treating me like a respectable older person who shouldn't be sexual. Well, I was a whole woman then, & I'm a whole woman now.

"She no longer has men, so she has God," Gustav Flaubert wrote to George Sand about their mutual friend. Am I just another middle-aged women substituting heavenly love for sexual love on earth?

Still, I am amazed at my new contentment, & play happily with these poems. (For, as exciting as some of these guys were, I've never loved a man more than I've loved a white page. This is still true, though my new snookie is as gorgeous & exciting as anyone in this book!)

Many names and some locations have been changed at the request of the pertinent fellow; the dates tend to be accurate.

With special thanks to the colleagues who suggested this collection: Marilyn Krysl, John Oliver Simon, and Julia Vinograd; to Kevin Flynn who has listened as only a friend can while I experienced these encounters; to Whitney Jones & Lynn Mandel for reading sections in various cafés, & to Jackson Dunckel for editorial advice which I sometimes followed.

& a kiss for Mark Steinbrink, who used to say, when I was an unknown housewife & he was a renowned dancer, "Will you still love me when you're rich & famous?"

alta

Berkeley • 1989

Contents

Moody Bitch with Attitude

Family

Friends

Lovers

HUSBANDS

Marriage is like a merry-go-round. I keep getting on different horses, but it's the same ride.

*female lions
have no mating
season. so the
males must be
able to perform
on the spot, for
any willing female.
loyalty is irrelevant.*

*still, the female must be
approached delicately. see
the male nuzzle her tummy.*

*this explains every one
of my marriages.*

Oakland • 1984

HONEYMOON

i smiled against your shoulder
as you carried me to bed.
the light of our lovemaking
can still be seen by stargazers
on other planets.

Logan, Oregon • 1962 • Bo

the clean warm trailer at night.
we hear the crickets & the crickets
hear us grunting & laughing. we
fill the room with lovesmells.

Logan, Oregon • 1962 • Bo

my husband's out
telling some woman
his wife doesn't understand him.

San Lorenzo • 1966 • Bo

FIVE YEARS LATER, I SPEND SIX WEEKS IN RENO

Too young, too soon, they
said. But we were so in love.
We didn't know what else to do,
with all that love.

Reno • 1967 • Bo

15

CONVERSATION WITH MY FIRST HUSBAND ON WHAT
WOULD HAVE BEEN OUR 25th ANNIVERSARY

Is this another swing to the depressive end of manic depression, or is there some comprehensible reason I can do nothing but cry? I look at the calender: this would have been our 25th anniversary. I call my first husband. "We made a terrible mistake, Bo."

"Which one."

"The divorce."

"You wouldn't have filed for divorce if I'd shaped up. I'm to blame."

"O, let's share the blame on this one. Lots of other women tough those things out; I thought there was a better life for me out there."

"Our whole generation was sold a bill of goods. They told us, 'You deserve the world!' & we chased after, & grabbed it, & we look back, where the hell did it go." He paused, then said, "As a young man, I was so theatrical! You knew I'd climb mountains for you, but I wouldn't say 'I'm sorry.' I'd swim rivers, but I couldn't say, 'forgive me.'"

"Everyone told us we were too young," I answer. "Also, I'd given up my work! That would cripple anybody. & then I demanded that you meet all the needs I'd created by capitulating."

"We thought there were rules to marriage. We were trying to abide by them. It wasn't until I met my present wife that I felt I'd ever know love again. But I do believe we can learn from the past; that we can use the mistakes of the past to make the future better," he said.

"Let's hope. Our kid has sure paid a heavy price for all our messing up." I start crying again.

"She's had a rough time, I know, but she's a lovely young woman nonetheless. I think you see all her anger; she's always on her good behavior with me."

"It's hard enough that we pay for our mistakes; it's really dreadful that others pay, too."

"We didn't just make mistakes. We had the kind of love you dream about. & they say, once you've known that, no one can take it away from you."

"Maybe that is true, Bo."

"I think so. I really think it is."

Berkeley • 1987 • Bo

16

I will show you
who you are
and what you
long for then
I will leave you

for I am a bird
you have seen me
many times
flying

you have longed
to follow me before
as you do now,
but it is not I
you must follow.

Berkeley • 1967

the nun walking
across the school yard,
her head bent.

you would turn to me
& laugh, & i would
close my eyes
to keep the beauty
of you in my mind.

it is difficult;
knowing you, &
doing without you.

Berkeley • 1967 • Simon

MENSTRUATION

i push my cramped belly
against your warm butt
you pat my hand & nod
& we sleep curled
into each other
and into ourselves.

Berkeley • 1968 • Simon

love,
the door opens without a key
& you walk to me, you're
hairy & brown & hard

when we hug it is always
my body that yields
(you've only got one soft place
& even that gets hard).

mansmell: sweat, woodsmoke,
printer's ink. i breathe deeply
& hold your hand to my cheek.

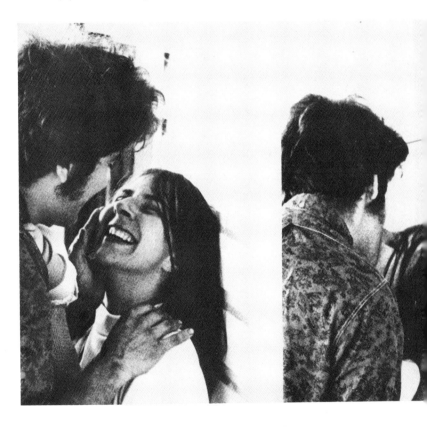

Berkeley • 1969 • Simon

FEATHERS ALL OVER THE FRONT ROOM

resentful, afraid
i turned you away tonight

warm dark neck
throat smooth to kiss

but my box feels zipped up
closed tight/ front to back

sorry, no one home
any woman can sew

Berkeley • 1970• Simon

RED SHIRT

there had been that intimacy between us.
i stood behind him; his body
had not lain in my arms for
two years. but our child was climbing
into the truck. there had been
that intimacy between us.

Berkeley • 1972 • Simon

"KEEP ME FROM THE OLD DISTRESS..."

- Dorothy Parker

I.

sitting at the candlelit table
is the beautiful woman who
uses her beauty like a key.
& once there, she
stands tall,
as if no one could
buy her at all.

she is constantly
in love, constantly
falling in love
she uses love like spice
& she can never get enough

if every hour were the approach
of a different lover, she would
feel neglected in the space
they took to change places.

she uses her beauty like a key.
& she turns men with her little key.
today there were four who wanted to be her lover.
she stares at the candle & wonders why
the beauty key only works with men
& why only the men come back for more.

she is the same person, is she not.
the same thigh touches the thighs of all
those who sit next to her.
she pushes the candle's wax drops in circles
on the table & prays that all those men
will add up to
one lover.

II.

why am i
never content.
broken lemon rind
on the white porcelain circle.
& the flowered bowl,
the vase,
the flame brighter than the marigolds.

& your hand curves over my breast like a shell
the green deep waters of your eyes
our bodies smooth as stones by water
& beneath your wet hair your surprisingly human
body with legs when all that time weren't we
leaping out & diving in / weren't we not quite
human in the green deep waters of our eyes?

San Lorenzo • 1971 • Angel

ooh i feel lika lil bee
makin off widda nectar

yr breath like irises,
yr open mouth a flower,
yr tongue ready in the center

& i feel lika lil bee
makin off widda nectar

San Lorenzo • 1973 • Angel

trying to comprehend aging, i
stare at new lines on my cheeks,
droopy skin on my neck.

angel strokes my back.
"i have always loved you, &
i have always found you beautiful."

Oakland • 1978 • Angel

My third husband
made an offer no poet
could refuse: all the
freedom I needed, &
all the sex I wanted.
He only turned me down
two times in ten years,
& one time, he was so ill
he was barfing into the toilet.
"Comeon, Angel."
"No, buns, I can't. It's BLUCH
not that I don't BLUCH love you, it's
just..."
"O, comeon, Angel. It'll help calm
your stomach."
"Really, BLUCH, buns, I just can't!
BLACH AGGH!"

Oakland • 1980 • Angel

27

WOMEN'S LIB HITS HOME

I used to do things like walk
in the house, sit down, look at Angel
& say, "My car battery is dead."

I could print a book;
swim a mile; I even
fixed the brakes on my volkswagen.

Still, as he came home
exhausted from work, I would
hit him with things like "The
basement is full of water."

Men could do things, I
thought. They really could! It's be-
cause of their big pee-pees.

Oakland • 1981 • Angel

DELUGED WITH DUDES

The sexual revolution came & went; my youth & beauty came & went; good timing.

DON

we were parked on a hill
warm in his blue chevvy.
he pulled me on his lap
his eyes closing with the
hot joy of it,
"o, sweets,
it never felt so good."

Castro Valley • 1958 • Don

That bitch Maretta won't get her arms
outta my face. I try running to the left,
but she's in front of me. Her arms are
as long as my legs. Corliss is in an open
spot, I bounce her the ball; Maretta turns &
Corliss whizzes it back to me. *Swoosh*
it's in. Kelly calls from the sidelines, "Go,
ALTA!"

He's our only spectator. No bleachers
for the girl's games, so he stands
for the two quarters I play.
We spend the other two seated
against the wall, he as proud
of me as I am of him, when he
plays forward, earning a sweater
for what the girls earn nothing for.

Castro Valley • 1959 • Kelly

my body was again a joy.
i felt myself coming
my inside walls pulsing hungry
for you.   all those months we were
together, i never yelled at the kids.

Berkeley • 1969 • B. K.

TO A MARRIED LOVER

I have no momento of you.
You bring me lips; hot nights
in the slick seats of cars.
You hold me in that old,
protective way.

When you go there is nothing.
It is as if we walked on the beach,
& forgot, in our joy, to pick up
even one piece of jade.

Richmond • 1977 • C. J.

JUST ANOTHER SEX POEM

"Why do you always want the lights on!" I reach over
& turn off the lamp.

"Why do you always want the lights off?" he replies,
& reaches over, & turns the lamp back on.

"Probably you being a slim 22 & me being a chubby
40 year old have an effect." I turn the light off again.

"That's not a good reason," he says. He kisses me
& turns the light on again.

Oakland • 1982 • Christopher

HARRY THE BIKER FROM ANTIOCH

He keeps looking at me; what the hell. I walk over
to his table, "Wanta dance?"
His buddy pushes him out of his chair, "Sure he does."
"Uh," says the biker, standing up, "I guess so."

He asks,"You're not one of them women's libbers, are you?"
"Bet your ass."
"Say what?"
"I said, you bet your ass I am."
Harry the biker from Antioch shrugs & says, "I can hang with that."

As I go down on him, he says, "Oh, baby. I never had a
woman treat me this way."
I look up, "You serious?"
"Well," he says, "not for free."

The next morning, he sees pictures of my kids. "You ain't older
than me, are you?"
"Probably. What are you, 30?"
"31."
"Yeah, I'm older. I'm 42."
"I can hang," says Harry.

We go to the cafe for breakfast, & I hand him a croissant.
"What the hell," he shouts, "this damn thing's empty! How much
you pay for this?"
"75c."
"Baby, you got ripped off. Don't never buy another one of
these things."

Oakland • 1984 • Harry

MR. NOT QUITE RIGHT & I WAKE MY ROOMMATE LYNN

"You've got breath like a dog's asshole, & you're telling *me* to lose weight?!" I'm ripping sweaty sheets off the bed, heaving pillows across the room. Billy's huddled naked in the corner, his hands over his balls.

I cram all his stuff in a bag & heave it outside. "Sleep in your car, dogbreath!" As I turn on the shower, I yell, "You know what Lorenzo said when I told him I'd lost ten pounds? *He* said, 'Baby! you gotta start eatin!'"

The next morning, I ask Lynn if we woke her. "Yeah, but you were just yelling, "Floss your moldy teeth, you motherfucker!" So I figured you were okay & I just went back to sleep."

Oakland • 1985 • Billy

37

WRONG NUMBER

"Hullo," he mumbles.
"Hi! This is Alta!"
"Say, baby!"
"Uh - "
"How you doin, sweetheart?"
"Maybe I have the wrong number."
"No, no, you got the *right* number!"
"No, I don't think I do, actually."
"Sure you do. I'm just wakin up, that's all."
"No, it's the wrong number. Sorry to wake you."
"Baby, honest, I remember you! Just remind me,
where'd we meet."
"Sorry, bye."
"O, girl, don't hang up! Comeon - "

Berkeley • 1986 • A friendly fellow

CLOSE BUT NO CIGAR

"There's two kinds of loneliness: loneliness with a man, &
loneliness without a man."

- Lorraine Hansberry

one street light a block away
dead end street houses all dark
wintercold outside / steam dripping down windshield
men's cologne on hairless cheeks
hard cheek bones, greasy hair
face pressed hard on my chest
please / no / please / no dont / i need you / no
big hands on my tiny tits *please*
             please
i would look at the monkey bites
later in my mirror & feel my cotton pants
all wet & feel cool clean sheets &
wonder who if ever & think
probably soon, probably somebody

Castro Valley • 1957 • Dale

JUST FRIENDS

I.

"Hey, you gonna write
a poem about me?" You
flash your eyebrows
at me. Sure, kid, I'll
writecha a poem. But
first, there's a couple
things I'd like you
to do...

2.

"You know scientists have discovered that smiling
makes you happy?:
"You mean the act of smiling,
without anything to be happy about?"
"Yep," you smile. "Even before I learned that,
I used to wag my dog's tail when he was depressed."
"Just pick it up & wiggle it back & forth?"
"Yep."
Bless our animal natures. You have the same effect
on *my* tail.

3.

I ask a question, & you give an
answer. What a treat.

(Only equals dare
tell each other the truth.)

4.

You wave from the café,
golden light on your
radiant face -
"We have lots of time!"
O, my young love, if only
that were true.

5.

Although I take a lover every spring & every fall
(I'm a human clock), this affair would hurt Angel;
he's met Michael, & knows that I spend
an evening a week with him. We decide
not to consummate our passion in order to
spare Angel pain. "But can we really
turn this down?" Michael asks.
"We're not puppets," I answer; "We can
make decisions in our lives."

Then I drive home the long way,
trying not to resent the man who has
loved me all these years, who is no
longer a door, but a wall.

Angel is sitting up waiting; he's even started
smoking again. As I walk in & kiss him,
he stares silently at me. "You look more beautiful
than I've ever seen you," he says quietly,
& I wonder what it cost him to say that.

6.

Postcard to Michael:

One day this month,
I had the old joy you
bring. My God, it
was a shock! The world
was too brilliant, almost,
to bear watching!

But I'm back to
normal now.

Oakland • 1978 • Michael

43

CUPID & PSYCHE

effortless as the
seine; inevitable
as sunlight

> *o, do*
> *not be deceived by*
> *his wings! he is a*
> *man, & has never*
> *flown! & with you, he*
> *has only the illu-*
> *sion of*
> > *(flight!)*

woman with white
skin, your touch cool
as marble, the
weightlessness of

> *Wings!*

the light across his
back, his perfect buns
how could she not reach
for him, who flew to her
unbidden; who
touched her as she had
not been touched in
too long a time.
how could she not
look up, & find him.
how could she hold only to
her wine jug, empty at
the end of each day?
how could she not
stroke the curls falling
into his face, into
her face, falling like light,
& the sound of wings.

Paris • 1980 • Michael

44

ORION

Orion
splayed out in the
sky over the mountain
over the highway

I stare at his belt; at
the three stars hanging
down/ a tasty nibble.
He knows I'm watching.

Every time I'm single,
he reveals himself.
What a patient suitor;
what a delicate approach!

Oakland • 1981

45

I'M SURE IT'S SOME KIND OF RECORD

One day I got stood up by 4 guys.
It started when I sat in the Med for an hour, waiting for
whatshisname to show up for breakfast. While I waited, I
chatted with friends, & when I told them it looked like
I was being stood up, we laughed.

After working a couple of hours, I went to Giovanni's to
meet whatshisname #2 for lunch. This was a tad embarrasing,
because I requested a table for two & ordered a bottle of
wine, which, as the hour went by, I proceeded to drink.

After a nap to sober up, I got to the pool just fifteen
minutes late to meet whatshisname #3. I decided I'd
swim til he came. I swam til they closed.

I went home & dressed for the party. Whatshisface #4
was to pick me up at nine. By this time, the day had begun to
take on the flavor of a zen exercise, so at 9:10
I called Karen. "Mercury's retrograde," she explained.
"That causes missed connections."
I did the dishes. Called Mom. Read a no-plot story in the
New Yorker. By ten I made a pot of tea & chugged around
the corner to the liquor store to buy a box of ginger snaps. I
changed back into my jeans & looked up my horoscope in
the Chronicle. Under Gemini it said,

> Be on your guard. Planned
> romantic interlude may fizzle.

Oakland • 1983 • Four useless sonsabitches

46

DRY SPELLS

"Horny men are like taxicabs: never there when you need them."

- Naked lady in *Penthouse*

At the motel in Fresno, I try to watch
the porno flick but my t.v. won't work.
Although it's midnight, the couple next door
is carrying on, full volume. The woman is
wailing OOH WAA! OOH WAA! & the man
starts uhn EE uhn EE

I decide to participate. "OOH WEE! OOH
WEE! I wish it was ME!" I shout
& a sudden silence falls.

Fresno• 1987

49

MY DRINKING BUDDY SHERRY

My drinking buddy Sherry was taking her divorce very hard. She kept muttering about how she'd cooked his favorite foods for five years, & for what. With her perfect complexion and silky red hair, she was used to multiple offers. Still, anyone can have a dry spell. It had been about three weeks for each of us, & we were getting creative. After another futile night in a bar in Hayward, we got in the car & were about to pull out when a guy tapped on my window. "You girls want a three-way?"

"O, no thanks. I hate that stuff." I smiled, & rolled up the window.

As he tottered off to his car, Sherry started in yelling at me, "Now you've done it! We finally get an offer, & you tell the guy no!"

"Well, you could've said something! He's right over there - let's go get him." I drove over toward his car. Having no idea of why we were rushing at him, he panicked & took off like a shot. I chased after, but he was really scared, & ran a couple of red lights.

Sherry was snarling, "Can't even catch him, you asshole." As we sat disconsolately in an all night diner, we decided the next night we should spend standing in front of a whore house with little signs saying **We don't charge**.

In order to prepare ourselves for this ridiculous endeavor, we spent the next evening drinking in Brennan's, during which an obnoxious frat boy wandered over & started making jokes. I laughed at one, & he turned to me, "O, I get it," he said, "You're the quick one."

When he went to the bathroom, Sherry asked, "Want to flip a coin?"

"This guy? He's all yours."

But she was nervous, having never done a one night stand before, & she insisted I go with them & sit in the other room.

It wasn't the best night I ever spent, but he had a great record collection, so it wasn't the worst, either.

Berkeley • 1981 • Sherry

50

MY HOROSCOPE PROMISED *THE END OF LONELINESS IS IN SIGHT: LOVE IS JUST AROUND THE CORNER.*

So I thot, okay,
& walked around
the block. Actually,
I did see one
beautiful man in a
tank top lounging
against the liquor
store. Muscular,
black shoulders
gleaming in the
sun. "Ooh, sweet
mama!" he called out.

Oakland • 1986

51

MOODY BITCH WITH ATTITUDE

Life's too short to drink bad wine.
                        - Italian proverb

Most women are shorter than
most men. It's easy to over
look us unless we stick our
fingers into yr eyes & say,
Look at me, buddy, or you
won't be able to see at all.

Berkeley • 1967

BITTER HERBS

Natural Pussy
25 cents in a dispenser
gulf station, pinole

j. douglas says prisoners
use cardboard rolls, filled
with a greasy baggie,
surrounded by a hot wet
                        washcloth
- sure feels like pussy.

playboy bunnies twitch their tails
bouncing squashedup titties
& grinning.

if you come in me
a child is likely to
come back out.
my name is alta.
i am a woman.

Berkeley • 1968

whatever your hangups dont hang em on me.
i dont carry daggers above my knee.
you want yr heart cut out? well, not by me.
dont hang yr hangups on me, not on me.

one man he loved me, he treated me good;
as long as i did what he thot i should.
next man was heavily intellectual; great
for conversation but we'd never ball.

i'm sayin i'm tired, i'm sayin i'm thru.
one man too many is one man like you.
keep yr old phonecall, keep yr old card:
buy yrself presents & be proud yr hard.

but i'm off on my own, friend, & i dont need you.
hang around with yr hangups, i'm sayin i'm thru.

Berkeley • 1970

MARRIAGE

it would be so easy to hand you my life
& say, here, i can't do it.
but my tense muscular arms would tremble
in their wedding rings

San Lorenzo • 1971

ABBREVIATED HISTORY OF AN INDEPENDENT WOMAN

1950: I do not have a husband.

1960: I do not have inhibitions.

1970: I do not have herpes.

1980: I do not have sex.

Oakland • 1985

59

FAMILY

"Tell them, Altie, tell them! We've been lied to from the cradle to the grave."

- My Father

CHAMPIONSHIP BRO

When Grandma died, I was 17. To comfort me
at the funeral, my little brother took my hand.

When I got married, Daddy couldn't face it,
so my brother walked me down the aisle.
By this time, he was 14.

When my older daughter started kindergarten,
I had a breakdown. I called my brother. He
came & made tea & sat with me as I lay in
bed, crying, until she came back home.

When my second daughter was born, my brother
came to help, and he made dinner for all the
neighborhood kids as well. They still ask
about him, 19 years later.

When I got famous, he arranged a reading for me
at his college. When I beat everyone at ping-pong
(including the local champion, my brother's
roommate Kenny, a gorgeous Chinese guy),
we all went dancing to celebrate my victory.

When I went through my second divorce, my brother
came over & took me out for dinner, promising to help
raise the children.

When my third husband tried to evict me from our house
after our divorce, my brother loaned me money to
buy him out.

When my older daughter was depressed, he paid
for a trip to Japan for her, a dream she had had
ever since our friends began teaching her
Japanese when she was seven.

When my younger daughter got accepted at the college he
had gone to, he spent an afternoon with her explaining the
the town, and the type of people thereabouts, & helped her
choose a more suitable college.

When I woke up from surgery last year, my brother was beside me,
holding my hand. May he live long & prosper. I've got the best
bro in the world.

Berkeley • 1989 • Bill Art

"CHILDREN PUT US ON EARTH."
-John Levy

Driving through the hills on a foggy day, listening
to the radio, we hear a woman sing about
being in heaven on earth.

Remembering that afternoon with Scottie, the sun
through the lace curtains, my fingers tangled
in his golden hair, I sigh, "I've known heaven on earth."

"Mother!" snaps my elder daughter, "That is *such*
a pedestrian concept!"

Berkeley • 1983 • Lori

WHEN KIDS COMPLIMENT YOU, IT'S NOT NECESSARILY FLATTERING

"I've decided you're not a slut." says my thirteen-year-old.
"You have?" I answer cautiously.
"Naw. You're just a lusty wench."
"Where do you get these phrases?"
She swaggers, "I'm an educated child."

Oakland • 1982 • Kima

Mom walks in to find me sobbing over some
transgression of husband #3. She tidies
up my kitchen, pats me, & says, "I never minded
my husbands' indiscretions."
"You didn't! Why?"
"Because," she smiles smugly, "Then they
forgave me my little peccadilloes!"

San Lorenzo • 1973 • A.P.

"We never had a
dime, Altie," Daddy

weeps, directing me to
find the fifty dollars by his

bed. "You go buy Momma
a pretty pin, now.

Something real pretty.
Now that we've got

money, & I'm
dying in this

sonofabitchin bed!"

Castro Valley • 1973 • Daddy

MY FIRST POETRY LESSONS

My first poetry lessons were from Cousin Charlie.

It all started when he decided to teach me
to say I was three instead of "Me free,"
which was what I had been saying.
This made Mom mad, since she loved
my baby talk, so to make up for it
he taught me all kinds of words
like *extrapolate*, & *agitate*, & then we'd
spend hours arguing about which words
sounded the prettiest.

It all ended when Charlie decided
that *tapioca* was absolutely the
prettiest word he'd ever heard,
& nothing I could say would ever top it.

Reno • 1945 • Charlie

68

FRIENDS

Interviewer: So you're looking for a grand passion?
Diane Sawyer: I've had grand passions.

He had invited me to a party. Hearing no music as I arrived, I asked, "Am I the first?"

"Now, don't be mad, Boobie. You & I don't need crowds or fancy places to have a good time, right? The barbeque is ready & I bought steaks"

"Have you had a couple of beers, Denny?"

"Couple. Maybe more than a couple." He put his arm around me, "Hey, here, have a beer."

"No one else is invited, is that it?"

"Well, yes, that's it. Listen, we'll have a bitchin time; here, take this beer. Take it!"

"Really, Dennis."

"& look. There's the pool table. We can have a game."

"Last time we had a game, I ripped the green."

He shakes his head, "Entirely my fault. Entirely my fault. There's this one little thing I forgot to show you." He pats my shoulder awkwardly, "You're not mad, hey? It'll be fine, believe me. Bitchin time."

I wore my green cashmere sweater & skirt, my long brown hair straight. I never wore heels with Denny because in 1960, the guys were supposed to look taller. He was wearing a new sports jacket I hadn't seen while we were seniors at Castro Valley High. At the dance, every girl there had a bubble haircut except me.

One of his frat brothers asked, "Are you in high school?"

Absolutely every girl there wore a black sheath with pearls. One girl asked, "Are you from out of town?"

On the way home, I told Denny I hadn't understood their questions. Were they being friendly, or had they intended to insult me? "Nah, no insult," he answered. "Dave, for instance: he thinks you're very pretty. Basically, he wants to get in your pants."

I believed him until the next frat party, where I overheard a skinny blond saying it was all very fine if Dennis wanted to be so loyal, but couldn't he get me a fashion consultant?

"Hey, Boobie! It's done!"

"Dennis, that's great! You actually built your own sailboat?"

"Impressed?"

"Of course I'm impressed!"

"So lemme take you out in it. How's Saturday?"

"Absolutely."

"I guess I should invite Hank too, hey?"

"O, pooh. He's always at practice on the weekends."

"Precisely why I should invite him. One, he could cream me

with his left hand, which he will, if he gets jealous; two, he won't be able to come but I'll come across like a good guy."

"Really, Dennis. You make him sound like Moose in the Archie comics."

But Denny invited us both, & Hank showed up to go sailing, & the boat tipped & we all tumbled into the bay. Dennis was apologizing like crazy, & Hank was laughing like crazy, & I just swam to shore.

As my roomie & I are looking up doctors in the yellow pages, Dennis calls. "Hey, Boobie. Hear you've got a problem."

"O, good; it's you."

"You should have told me yourself. Why didn't you?"

"Well, it's neither your fault nor your problem."

"Very heroic. Listen: we could get married; that way, the baby would have a name. & after it's born, you could get a divorce if you wanted; I wouldn't stand in your way."

"Denny, you're so sweet."

"See? You could finish the semester, & we could get an apartment, heck, I could help you with your physics!"

"You told me you flunked physics."

"What are you talking about? I got a B & it was the honors class! You're the one who's flunking physics!"

"Just a moment. Tony's at the door."

"*Tony*? He'd make a *terrible* father!"

"I'm not going to marry him, dingdong! He's taking me to the movies."

"Well, think about this, okay?"

"Thanks for the call, Denny. I really appreciate this."

"You're not saying yes. Do you love the father?"

"No."

"So even if you tell him, you wouldn't marry him."

"No."

"Well, let's do it, Boobie. I'd do my best to take care of you. Heck, I even like kids!"

"Denny, I can't. I'll never forget this, but I just can't get married right now. I'm only nineteen!"

"Hey, hey, don't cry. I swear, people get through this all the time. The world's full of babies! Don't cry, Boobie; just marry me. You know I cook a mean steak."

"Bless you, Denny. Thank you. But no."

After graduation, Denny got married. I wore black. His mother kissed me in the reception line, so I felt suddenly guilty & said, "Perhaps I shouldn't have worn black."

She smiled, "It's sort of touching, dear." His dad shook my hand & asked what my real name was, since he didn't want to introduce me to people using Denny's nickname for me, which was understandable.

Denny hugged me & introduced me to his wife; a very pretty woman, small & dark.

Ten years later, my ex-husband Bo stopped by. As I poured tea, I asked, "Remember Dennis?"

"Hell, yes! How is old Denny?"

"He's dead. He was in an accident a year ago."

Bo was silent a moment, then he said, "Do you hate me?"

"No, why?"

"Tell me a thing like that."

"I thought you'd want to know."

"No way. No way would I ever want to know that a friend like Denny had died."

I never thought it would happen to me. For years, I've heard that middle-aged men prefer younger women, but I always assumed I'd be immune; that the pestering would continue. I've heard how women my age end up alone; either by choice, like Jennifer, or because they feel they have no choice, like Nancy. But men seem to be ageist as well as sexist. After reading the ads by women in the New York Review of Books, where they all claim to be unique, and hearing that in my age group it's six single women for every single man, I decide to stop searching for someone appropriate & be glad Lorenzo pays periodic visits.

The only social life I've had lately is my work. You could explain all this, Denny, & tease it away. It's been twenty years since you've called. Is that anyway to treat your old Boobie? Whaddya say. Stop being dead, Denny, & come over for a beer.

Castro Valley, Berkeley • 1960, 1987 • Dennis

73

ADVICE I INTEND TO FOLLOW AS SOON AS POSSIBLE

The owner of my favorite café pays a rare visit
to town; I ask him to make me a cappucino for
old time's sake. He smiles, "How are you, Alta."
"O, Lino. I'm old & fat."
He winks, "Go to Italy!"

Berkeley • 1981 • Lino

THE BEST THING ABOUT GETTING OLDER IS YOU GET SO SUAVE

A tall blond walks toward me. Ooh, goody,
it's my gorgeous Pac-man coach! "How's it going?"
he shouts, & I immediately fumble & drop a full
glass of orange juice. But, hey, I catch it,
without spilling a drop! I look up at him &
he winks, "Good catch."

The student that Christopher nicknamed
Joe Atlas is walking up the steps toward
the café. He's wearing nothing but a tank top
& shorts. I decide today is the the day I will treat him
as just another human being, so when he smiles
& asks, "Hi, Alta; how're things?" I smile calmly
back, "Fine, thanks." & walk into a tree.

Berkeley • 1985 • Paul / Mark

75

I visit a young friend in Madrid; he's concerned that his current girlfriend is more sophisticated than he.

"In my experience," I begin,

"Which is considerable," he interjects,

"...it takes three things to make a great lover: enthusiasm, affection, & technique."

He brightens, smiles, & sits up straighter. "Hey! I've got two out of three!"

Madrid • 1985 • J.D.

76

My student Zach & I are having one of our public arguments. I've just told him that without the women's movement, I'd probably be dead, because I couldn't stand my life as a young woman, & was repeatedly suicidal.

"That's so stupid!" he shouts. "A white woman in an iron lung has an easier life than a young black man in the United States!"

"Everyone feels that their own pain is the most real, the most severe," I say. "I wasn't trying to win an oppression contest, I just couldn't stand my life at that time."

"God, that would have been so selfish of you!" he shakes his head. "Where would I be now if you'd died?"

The kids in town call me Big Al. During one confrontation, the boy who's been accused of rape stares down at me, & mutters, "Big Al ain't so big."

A flash of fear, then I straighten. I see Zach behind him, watching carefully. I look back at this baby jock & say, "She's big enough."

I'm happily playing with my poems, but wonder aloud if I should be dealing with reality instead, since there are so many home-less kids around town. Zach shakes his head. "The greatest thing you can do for another human being is to tell their story."

I wrap the shirt he gave me around my shoulders, like a prayer shawl. For twenty years, runaway youngsters & homeless kids have been landing on my porch, waiting to see if I'll take them in. Some people attract cats.

I send one kid back to her parents after an interesting but strenuous five weeks. Immediately, there are two other kids who want her room.

I discuss everything with Zach. He likes one guy because he's trying to break away from his rough past. I like him too, but his brother makes me nervous.

He also likes the white student who has a keyboard that Zach could play when he makes up songs.

My younger daughter suggests redesigning the apartment so that we could fit another futon on the floor; maybe one kid could sleep in the storage room.

O, who knows. It's my life. My miraculous, bizarre life of loving & resisting love.

Berkeley • 1989 • Zach, & assorted young lions

77

Spence calls & I take all my current nastiness out on him. He answers, "Hey, hold it. Why don't you just tell me three things that are bothering you right now."

I think for a moment, then say, "I've got another godamned rash, so my hands are covered with itchy bumps; all the men my age are desparately trying to find women still young enough to have babies, & I don't have enough money to pay the phone bill."

"Okay. One at a time: itchy bumps are nothing to worry about, men aren't *worth* worrying about, & money comes & goes."

When I laugh, he says, "Now that we've solved something, how about dinner Thursday?"

But just because he made me laugh doesn't mean things are solved. I snarl, "So that I can pay for it? Terrific!"

There's a startled silence, then he says quietly, "Actually, I get paid on Wednesday. That's one of the reasons I suggested Thursday."

A couple of hours later, I'm feeling contrite. I call him back. Oops, he sounds sleepy. "Sorry to wake you, " I say.

"It's okay. You feeling better?"

"Actually, I'm calling to apologize for being so bitchy when you called earlier. It feels like all I've done today is make mistakes."

"No, no, my dear." I hear him lighting a cigarette. "Don't apologize. Besides, between us, there's no such thing as a mistake."

San Francisco • 1988 • Spence

78

THE MARTY POEMS

Tired from coping & worrying over the future,
I mumble, "Life takes constant courage."
Marty turns toward me. "That's why
it's so important to live so that
you're not ashamed of yourself. It's hard
enough already."

Oakland • 1981 • Marty

MARTY TEACHES ME THRASH DANCING WHILE I
TEACH HIM POETRY

"Poets are, by nature, religious, because what we're doing
is exploring creation." Mart doesn't answer; he's whizzing
around the front room, whapping at me with his elbows.
 "We listen," I go on, "To the voices of 'animate' &
'inanimate' beings, recording their information." Still no
answer. His eyes are shut, he's whooshing all around
the room. "You listening, or what."
"Course I'm listening!" he huffs, leaning over to turn up the music.
"Catch this dude, Altie...dadadada WOOOOOOOOOOO!"

Oakland • 1981 • Marty

I mention to Jackson how good Marty smells.
"He's seventeen," Jackson waves his arms, "All seventeen
year olds smell like honey!"

The next day, Mart asks me, "How am I gonna get that girl
to go out with me, Alta."
"Just let her stand down wind from you."

Oakland • 1983 • Marty/ Jackson

Jackson & I are lounging in a sunny café. He sighs happily, "All breasts are beautiful!"

The young couple at the next table are arguing: she wants a nose job, & he's trying to convince her it's unnecessary. "Listen," he leans forward, "I love you, right? I'm not going to love you more if you have a little nose!"

I whisper, "You should tell her all noses are beautiful, too, Jackson."

"I *knew* you wouldn't let that drop!" he whispers back.

But the boy is continuing his argument, "& if you're worried about what would happen if we break up, & how other guys might feel? Look at this woman behind me!"

Jackson & I look at each other. The woman behind him is me.

The boy whispers, "She's got a nose you wouldn't believe, right?" The girl shifts a little to sneak a peak. I decide to play, & turn my head so she can see it in all its glory.

She looks again at the guy. "Yeah?" she whispers back.

"Well. You should see the guy *she* goes out with!"

I nudge Jackson, "He can't be talking about Harold."

"I shouldn't think so."

Mart whizzes by on his skateboard & tosses a dollar at me. He shouts, "Hey, Altie! Get me a mocha!"

The boy whispers to the girl, "See?"

"Wow!" she whispers back.

"O, for Christ's sake!" I snarl. "Even these *kids* think Mart & I are having an affair!"

"SHHH!" Jackson covers my mouth. "You are being granted the opportunity to save a beautiful young girl's nose!"

Berkeley •1984 • Marty /Jackson

82

MART GIVES ME HALF HIS JELLY BEANS, PLUS
ALL THE BLACK ONES

"You ever hear about Saint Anthony, Mart? He went into the
desert cause he was tired of distractions; he was gonna
consider only the big questions."
"Yeh?"
"For twenty years, all he had were sex dreams."
"Hah!"
"Well, so, I've done the opposite."
"What, screwed around for twenty years & had spiritual insights?"
"Exactly."

Oakland • 1983 • Marty

Mart calls up. "Can I bring a friend to see you?"
"I suppose. What's happening."
"Well, I figure he needs somebody to talk to."
"Yeah?"
"Thing is, he got raped."
"O, no."
"So can we come over?"
"Sure. Anything specific I should do?"
"Just be there."

The boy huddles in a chair, silent as I pour tea. Mart & I make
occasional statements about various things.
When the boy wanders over to the bookcase, I mutter, "It's
another problem we can't solve, Mart."
"Anyways, we're here for him to turn to. That's more than some
folks have."
"True."

Oakland • 1984 • Marty

84

MARTY & I TAKE A BUSINESS TRIP TO BEL AIR

1.
I call my older daughter at college; tell her Marty's the best
male travelling companion I've had since Philippe &
Dominique. She laughs, "I can just see you two, giggling your
way through the L.A. freeway system."
"I guess Mart & I do have an unusual relationship."
"It's unheard of! That's why people are so rude about it."

Spence is annoyed that folks think he & his best friend are gay. I
tell him some of the cracks people have said to Marty & me.
"You know what it is?" he muses. "People don't comprehend
simple affection. They expect people to be useful, & to use
each other. Maybe it's part of a consumer society; we're even
supposed to consume human beings."

2.
I cut my date with the pilot short to rush back to take Mart out on
the town. He refuses to leave the hotel room. "No way," he
snarls. "I've watched three lousy shows while you were out with
that dude; this is the first good movie. I'm not going anywhere!"
Annoyed & disappointed, I go to bed. As I drift off to sleep,
Mart yells, "Hey! Wake up! Here comes this great scene -
watch, wouldja! Come on, Altie, wake up! The dog's face is
about to melt!"

3.
I feel a tug at my hand, his gentle voice, "You can't write in your
sleep, silly." & he takes the pen, clears the convention
catalogues off my bed, turns out the light & tiptoes away.

4.
"Mart, get up."
"What time is it."
"Seven. The book exhibit opens at nine."
"Seven? I've only had three hours of sleep!"
"I didn't make you stay up to watch *The Thing.*"
"Go away."

After swimming, I return to find him still asleep.
I uncover his foot, & yank him onto the floor. He
swats at me, "This is NO WAY to treat a young man
with hair on his chest!"

Bel Air • 1984 • Marty

WE VISIT A POET & PONDER LIFE

We visit Mitsuye; she's been married to Yosh for 34 years. As we drive away, Marty notices my silence & asks, "Regretting your past again?"
"You know, I've always maintained that my husbands pulled unforgivable stunts, but perhaps - it could be my own restlessness that killed those relationships."
"Well, you know what happened to me & Robin."
"I forget."
"She was really important to me. But spring came, & my hormones went on a rampage."
"Ah."
"& she was really special. It wasn't just sex with her."
"Yeah. Scott was the greatest lover, but when I turned 40, I just went after everyone that was still alive." We drive along the freeway, staring silently at the cars ahead, & at our unloving past behavior.

"You know what it is?" I start thinking out loud, "I've swallowed the poet's religion of GO FOR IT! The religion of experience. But it's not the only way to go, plus which, it's exhausting. Plus, it ignores all the pain that living like that causes other people: all the women who spend a month crying because you've run off with their husband for an unforgettable week in Carmel except in about ten years, you can hardly remember the dude's face!
"& these self-vindicating poets don't tell you how to survive this lifestyle. 'Go for the peaks,' they give you that part of the map, but they don't warn you about the long slide down, & some of them die, because they don't know, any better than the rest of us, how to cope with sorrow & pain."
"You do go for the peaks & valleys," he agrees. "As if the only other choice were the plains. But hey, Altie, there's also the foothills!"

"On the other hand, Mart."
"Yo."
"My first husband drank, & a couple of times he socked me."
"Yeah?"
"So I was right to get out of that."
"Of course you were! Who said you weren't?"
"Mom said I caused his alcoholism."
"Hardly."
"& then the next one dislocated my jaw."
"Not that nice guy from New York?"
"Right. & you know the one I just divorced."
"O, yeah. I hope not all men are like your husbands, Alta."

"Well, so, restless or not, I think I was right to get out of those relationships. I have met women who stick it out through all those situations, though; I guess I could have tried that."

"Not your style."

"I had to drag the kids through those divorces, go on welfare, go hungry, but by God, I walked away from those men."

Marty nods, "It was historically the first time possible. When ever before in the world, have women been able to leave their personal oppressors & survive?"

ADVICE I DECIDE NOT TO TAKE

Bill, who's always lusting after teenaged boys,
is urging me to screw Marty. "Comeon, dearie;
every young man needs an older woman!"
　　"Not for sex," I counter.
　　"Look at him! He's incredible! Why not
go for it?"
　　"Listen, Bill. This town's full of gorgeous dudes.
But how often can you find a good secretary?"
　　He nods. "Ah. Yes. You have a point, there."

Berkeley • 1984 • Bill / Marty

Fighting with my daughter again, I have no guidelines. I call old Mart. "What's up, Altie."

"My kid's at a party & they're drinking."

"Yeah?"

"I want to go get her."

"That would be a bad move."

"Really?"

"Really. Consider: you would embarrass her in front of her peers; you'd infringe on her social life, plus you'd be saying, 'you can't cope with this.'"

"But she shouldn't be there, Mart! It's all older kids."

"The only reason you know that she's there is because she called & told you, right? & she must have told you what's going on, as well."

"Right."

"Don't close that channel."

"O, god. What do I do?"

"Tell her tomorrow - not tonight - that you don't like it. Make sure she knows she can always call for a ride home, so a bunch of drunk kids aren't in a car. & if you feel it's necessary, do some discipline thing."

"Like put her on restriction?"

"Something. But not totally out of line; just enough to let her know you care, and that you don't want her in those situations."

I ponder this, then say, "But Mart. It's such a rough crowd!"

"Rougher than your crowd? Than my crowd?"

"Ah."

"She has to learn, too, Altie. But do talk to her tomorrow."

"Right."

"& try not to panic. At least she knows you love her. Why don't you visit Jackson tonight. Or go to a café. Do something to help yourself through this." Then he chuckles gently, "It's kind of dear, though, Altie. You're acting just like a mommy."

Oakland • 1983 • Marty

89

"Kerouac had this great prayer that he taught Gary Snyder. It goes something like, 'Gary Snyder, part of the void, part of the process, on his way to Buddhahood.'"

"He'd pray that way for Snyder?"

"Actually, he prayed that way for everyone in his circle, starting with his loved ones, then his friends, then his enemies. Trying not to feel either great love or great hate as their names flashed by. It helps, if you're trying to be holy, to see people in process. I tend to think of them as finished products. Anyhow, while I'm wandering in the mountains, this prayer might be good to ponder."

"Go to Kelso," he suggests. "There's this huge sand dune, big as the Berkeley hills, but all sand."

I hand him the map so he can circle it. "You know what the Hindus call this period I'm going through?" I ask him. "*The Flowering Tree.* Sarcastic sons of bitches."

"They probably do it on purpose. You know, to keep your spirits up."

"Aah. I've done so many harmful things. Caused so many divorces. It's only karmic that I have this fierce loneliness to go through."

"Well, okay," he pauses, "but remember, you're in process too."

The prayer as reported in THE DHARMA BUMS reads, "Japhy Ryder, equally empty, equally to be loved, equally a coming Buddha."

Berkeley • 1984 • Marty

LOVERS

"Sex is good for about two years, & then you need love."

- Zsa Zsa Gabor

after that ballplayer in new york,
(but o! what a red pick-up truck he
had!) i swear, NO MORE younger men.
then came you.

Oakland • 1981 • Scott

WE GO PUBLIC

"I think that's terrific!" beams the white-haired grandmother at
the company dinner. "Don't be embarrased: it's terrific that
you're the one paying for dinner with your credit card."
    "I'm afraid people will think he's my gigolo," I whisper.
    "Listen," she leans forward, "Screw people. What a privilege,
to be with a man just because you want to!"

At the fancy art opening, Scott walks
past three beautiful models to bring me
the biggest piece of chocolate cake.
One of them giggles.
He bends to kiss me, "Here
you go, my leetle dumpling,"
he rumples my hair, & wanders
off in search of wine.

Dublin • 1982 • Scott

94

ROAD TRIP

Returning from Sonoma, tired & hungry, Scott & I argue for fifty miles. Finally I decide this is stupid, & pull over. "Do you want to fight?"

"No."

"Me neither." I reach to hug him & he slips his hand down my pants. We can't do much on the off ramp, so we drive on. As cars whiz past, he tries to undress me, & diddles away. I can't concentrate on driving, & pull off again. We are in Petaluma; tract housing. Great. Just like high school; I look for a dead-end street with no lights.

We get comfortable and begin. I hear a car door. "Dear. Isn't that a car door?"

"Yup."

"Might be a cop."

He lifts his head from between my thighs, "Tell him I can't talk now; I'm busy."

I hear another door. "That was another door, dear."

"Yup. House door."

"Think so?"

"Know so. People drove home, went in their house. Happens all the time." We carry on; he urges me, "Come on, relax. You know nothin's gonna happen til you relax."

"Maybe those people noticed us."

He sits up, looks around. "Nah. Nobody around. I see the car; it's in that driveway across the street. & the house is all dark; they've just gone to bed."

"You sure?"

"Sure I'm sure. It's the middle of the night! Now *relax*, wouldja?" After what seems like ages, I finally come, & nestle into his lap to return the favor.

After awhile I rise & kiss him. The porchlight across the street flashes on. We stare. Four teenagers come out & wave & cheer. "O, Jeez," I moan, frantically trying to start the car. "Where's the frigging ignition?" Scott rolls down the window & waves at the happy onlookers.

"Did you know that whole time?" I hiss, driving away in the dark since I'm too embarrased to turn on the head- lights.

"I knew, if you thought anyone had seen us, you'd never come!" He kisses my ear, "Ah, my leetle dumpling! It is better for them to see two people in love than to watch a violent t.v. show, don't you think?"

Petaluma • 1982 • Scott

95

STRESS CITY

My ex-husband is trying to evict us on the grounds that since his income is ten times what mine is, he owns more of the house. My lawyer Gerald assures me we won't lose ("He would have to get past me, Alta, & there's just no way!"), but I'm scared anyway.

Driving north to do a performance, my cheap car breaks down & gets towed away as junk. The junkyard pays me $50. This will not replace my car.

Since I'm late for the perfomance, they put me at the very end of the program, & cut my pay nearly in half.

I solve these problems by yelling at Scott for six hours.

As we climb into bed, he reaches for me & I swat him. "O, no, you don't!" I grab my pillow & my dolly & stomp out to the couch, where I lay crying, furious that he's not coming to comfort me. What the hell kind of man lets a woman lie on the couch, crying.

I get up to make tea & he peeks in at me. "Don't even try it, sonofabitch!" I snarl. He retreats silently. What kind of man retreats when you yell at him. Fuck him, he's useless. I sit in the cold kitchen, sipping the tea.

Once my tummy is full of tea & cookies, it occurs to me that basically, Scotty hasn't done anything wrong. Maybe I could lie next to him.

I sneak back into bed, arrange my pillow & my dolly. He opens his arms & I curl against his chest. I mutter, "Sorry I bitched at you for six hours."

"Ah, my lettle dumpling." He strokes my hair, "you were entitled."

Oakland • 1982 • Scott

JUDY COMES TO VISIT

Judy asks, "You
don't have those
wrinkles on the back
of your neck, do you?"
Alarmed, I ask,
"What wrinkles?"
Scott slaps the table.
"Give us a *break!*
Don't give her
something new
to worry about!"

The next day, he
catches me staring
at my wrinkles. He
grabs my hand &
stomps out, pulling
me along. "STOP
this crap!" he shouts.
"Work on your spiritual
development!"

Oakland • 1983 • Scott

AN INOPPORTUNE PHONE CALL

Corinne calls, frantic & overworked. "Is Angel living with his girlfriend?"

"Yep. He seems pretty happy."

"How old is she?"

"I dunno. Maybe 25. Can I call you back?"

"Isn't that horrible."

"Huh?"

"How do you feel about that?"

"What?" I swat at Scott, who's busily biting my right bun.

"My exhusband has some young chippie..."

"O, well," I say, twirling Scotty's hair around a finger. "Springtime. Babies. Gonads. You know."

"I can't stand it that he's with a younger woman!" she shouts into the phone.

"Comeon, Corinne. Your snookie can't be more than 30."

"That's true," she giggles.

Scott's trying to pull off my pants. "Hang up," he mutters.

"Can I call you back? I'm in the middle of something." I'm trying to breathe normally into the phone.

"Well, how do you feel about Angel & that woman?"

I diddle Scott's nipple. "Tellya what. On one of those glorious October nights I was watching Scottie's blond hair between my legs & I decided, 'Who cares if Angel's happy? I just don't want to waste my time being miserable.'"

Scott shouts, "WIll you tell that broad to HANG UP?" & lunges for the phone.

"Bye, Corinne. I'll call tomorrow."

Scott whams down the phone. "Dang! Don't you have any polite friends?"

Berkeley • 1983 • Scott

WEIRD NIGHT`

He's in the kitchen, jabbing at his stomach with the butcher knife, shouting that I don't really love him, all I want is sex. I get the knife away from him & run outside. He chases me, knocks me down in a yard up the street. As I fall, I cry, "Call the cops!" Lorenzo's grandma opens her window, reassures me, "They've already been called."

Three of my friends got beat up that night by their husbands. Clark went after Connie with a broken bottle, José gave Janet a black eye, & Leonard yanked out some of Carol's hair. We all met in the café the next day, & said, "What the *hell* is going on!"

As we were pondering this weirdness, Scott came in on crutches, & the other three women whooped & cheered. Connie nodded, "Good for you, Alta." But she decided to divorce Clark rather than learn self-defense.

Oakland • 1983 • Scott

99

FOUR POINT PROGRAM FOR DEALING WITH AN ABUSIVE LOVER:

1. Change the lock.

2. Move them into a place of their own, even if I have to loan them the rent money.

3. Never be alone with them when they're drunk.

4. I've already studied karate & knife fighting; this time I take tai chi.

Oakland • 1983 • Scott

AFTER TWO WEEKS OF WILLPOWER, I BRING YOU HOME

our kisses so deep; your
cock so stiff inside me -

yes. i understand why
janet stays with josé;
why carol has not
left leonard. yes.
kiss me / yes

women are only
human / yes / love
is our bread, lust
our jam.

Oakland • 1984 • Scott

no, he is not the most
peaceful lover i ever
held. but he brought me

happy dreams. that
was the secret part, the

clean part. the smooth
manzanita of our
love.

Oakland • 1985 • Scott

yes, we chipped away / but
no statue blossomed.

only lovers / crawling with
ecstasy/ only those

moments, heat & sweat
all the smells of love

& the wet beds / but
no peaceful linking

of the day to night/
a common journey. still,

every woman should know
such passion, once

just to prove to herself
that dreams do not lie.

that young men, who charge
like bulls, & caress like

wings are not figments,
nor poetic fragments

but live, thrashing legs
& voracious mouths.

Oakland • 1984 • Scott

LORENZO

Karen stops by. "My dear, you're
positively glowing!" Lorenzo
walks thru & waves at her.
She says, "Isn't that Ruby's son?"
"Um-hmm. He mows my lawn."
"I see," she nods. "& how often
does he, ah, mow your lawn?"

Oakland • 1985 • Lorenzo

Lorenzo gets offered a job in the white folks town of Lafayette. He asks if I can drive him there a day early so he can scope the place out.

I wait half an hour, then decide to go to hear the Coasters with Lynn. Lorenzo comes up as we're leaving. "Hey, baby! You drivin me?"

"Too late, pal. We're going to a concert."

He throws his cigarettes on my lawn, "Property & society! Society & property!"

Although he gets the job, the army recruiter keeps calling. Lorenzo agrees to see her. I tell him it's dangerous, but looking at the knife wounds on his back, I realize his old neighborhood is probably as dangerous as the army.

Still, I'd rather have him alive & well, & so I say, "It's fine with them if you end up dead, you know."

He nods, "There's a genocide campaign against the black man."

"If you feel that way, don't go!"

"Baby," he puts his hands on my shoulders, "I'm a bus boy. I work for tips. Can you hear me?"

Oakland • 1985 • Lorenzo

"Neighbors tell me they ain't seen Willie around."

"Sonofabitch told me to lose weight. You know those ten pounds it took me months to lose? I've gained every one of them back!"

"That's cause your mind be sayin one thing, & your will be sayin the other. Your mind be sayin, okay, I can handle it/ but your will be sayin, ain't no motherfucker gonna tell me what to do!"

I stare down at my tummy.

"Hey. Come here, babe." He reaches for me, "Lemme put my arms around you here..." he hugs my hips; "& here," he hugs my chest, "& here," he hugs my waist. "See? You fit in my arms just fine."

Oakland • 1985 • Lorenzo

IT'S NOT THE SIXTIES ANYMORE

At the clinic, I learn I have v.d. again. I decide to break up with all five of my lovers.

I tell Lorenzo.

He shakes his head, "Just give me the medicine, baby. This it?"

"Well, yes, but..."

He pops it in his mouth. "There. How long it take?"

"Coupla days."

"See you Saturday." He kisses me & leaves.

Lynn sees Lorenzo on the porch. "I thought Alta broke up with everybody," she says.

"Um-hmm."

"Not you, though?"

"Yeah. Me too."

"So what are you doing here?"

"She tempermental," Lorenzo explains. "She break up with me Monday, I be back Tuesday. She *still* be mad, i wait a week."

"*Now* why won't you give me no poo," he complains.

"Diseases."

"I took the medicine, I get the blood test, & we use condoms! Woman, what you want!"

"I think we should break up. Condoms just cover the bottom part. We might catch something from kissing."

"We won't kiss."

"But that's my favorite part! I *love* kissing you while you're inside me!"

"I got condoms in my glove compartment: I'll wear two on my dick & one on my tongue!"

Oakland • 1985 • Lorenzo

107

Lorenzo returns from a construction job out of town. "How's the neighborhood."

"Terrible! Do you know five guys were killed around here last year?"

"Poverty," says Lorenzo. "You read all the wars in the papers, think, that's terrible. Then you drive home, see the neighbors fightin, that's worse. Then you walk in your house & your heart start to hurt, cause you know you brought the war right in with you."

Oakland • 1987 • Lorenzo

THE *I CHING* SAYS <u>DANGER</u> BUT I SEEM TO BE IN LOVE ANYWAY

I haven't wanted another man since Lorenzo told me he loves
me. This is so bizarre, I call Jennifer for a reality check. She
laughs, "HAH! You're in the soup now, kid!"
    "I shoulda known better than call you for sympathy."
    "Listen, kid, men grind you to dust. But *you* waiting at *home?*
HAH! Talk about karmic debt!"
    "O, shove it."
    "No, no, I don't mean to be harsh. He hee. But better you
than me!"

My Pac-man coach sees me sitting alone again on Saturday
night. "You still with Lorenzo?"
    "Yeah."
    "Have you told him yet you don't go out with anyone else?"
    "No."
    "I think you should tell him."
    "Aah. Besides, he might not care."
    "Sure he would. How long have you been monogamous
now?"
    "Two years," I whisper, looking around.
    He smiles, "That's okay. I won't tell anybody. Why are you,
though?"
    I shrug, "Fear of diseases."
    Paul shakes his head. "I don't believe that."
    "Why not?"
    "You're being monogamous, but Lorenzo isn't, & you know it.
If disease were the only reason, you would have broken up
with him by now."
    "I break up with him all the time!"
    "Comeon. What's the real reason."
    "O, balls! Because I don't *want* anybody else! Now was
that so important to hear?"
    "Yes, it was to me. I wanted to hear that."
    "Why?"
    "Because that's what I figured anyway, & because I hope
that someday an independent woman will love me that much,
& because it's neat." I laugh, & he says, "Love is never anything
to be ashamed of. It doesn't mean you're a fool: is that what
you're afraid of?"
    "I don't know what I'm afraid of."
    "He loves you, too. I mean, two years! He's never been with
anybody else that long, right? Although," he says, fishing in his
pockets for change, "I can see how these Saturday nights
might be hard to take. You want an espresso?"
    "Sure."
    "But tell Lorenzo. This is really a silly thing to lie to him about."

Someone's banging on the door, middle of the night. I go downstairs in a robe, look through the glass to see Lorenzo. He's drunk & wild-eyed. The usual story: some guy, some fight, he needs money.

"Forget it, Lorenzo. You know not to come here when you're drunk." I fish out four quarters & shove them at him.

"Aw, baby, this all you got?" He tries to hugs me, stumbles. "Here. It's okay. Give me a hug."

I nudge him back outside. He shakes his finger at me, "I'll be back. I'm serious!"

"Don't bother, Lorenzo. I'm serious, too." It's a promise I made when I was 24, & I've kept it; I never intend to live with an alcoholic again.

He's down the steps, wandering off to find his friend. I reassure myself, "I didn't cause it, & I can't cure it." But I'm frightened & lonely, & I cry before I fall asleep.

Berkeley • 1988 • Lorenzo

I've always promised Momma she can die at home. But her nurse comes over to find her sitting in the middle of the floor, confused & dirty. The nurse calls an ambulance, & the doctors put Momma into a rest home.

I spend the weekend in guilt & sorrow. Although Lorenzo & I haven't screwed since that drunk scene, he calls to ask how Momma is.

A few days later, he calls collect & I accept the call. "Can I borrow five bucks?" he wants to know.

"Sure. In fact, you can borrow ten."

"What happened."

"Two things. One, I've been dating this middle-aged white dude; single father, nice guy."

"Yeah?"

"He thinks sex is too much trouble."

"He still alive?"

"Second, you're the only friend who called to see how Momma is. You're reinstated. You can have anything you want."

"Really?"

"Try me."

His voice gets lower, "Can I have some of that sweet nookie?"

"Probably. Yeah, sure."

"Really? Can I move in?"

"Umm. Lemme think about it."

"Goddamn! I *am* reinstated!" As I laugh, he says, "Hey, you laughin? O, did I make you laugh? O, that's good to hear! I love you, Alta."

"Love you too, Lorenzo."

Berkeley • 1988 • Lorenzo

111

Doctors keep telling me to lower my stress.
I tell them if they knew what I was going through,
they wouldn't say something so stupid. Finally, one
says, "I can't change your life, & maybe neither can
you. But you can take some time for yourself every
day - take half an hour to do something you love to do."

Lorenzo calls, "Come pick me up."
    "I'm working."
    "Come pick me up, & after we have an hour at the hot
tub, go back to work."
    "Can't."
    "Too much to do?"
    "Yup."
    "Remember what the doctor say. You got a pencil
in your hand?"
    "Yeah."
    "Put it down." He pauses, "did you put it down?"
    "Yeah."
    "That was the hard part. Now come get me."

When I pick him up, he climbs in the car muttering, "What a day.
What a day." He takes me to Wendy's for lunch & as we sit by
the park eating stuff I don't eat with anyone else in the world, he
says, "You look like you been through world war three, baby.
What the problem?"
    "Eh." I shrug.
    "Comeon, baby. We talk. I ain't just your lover, I'm your
friend. What is it."
    I just start crying. He takes my hamburger & puts it on the
dashboard & pulls me into his arms. "Okay, now. Okay. We
talk."
    Finally I manage to tell him my daughter moved out.
    "She run away?"
    "No."
    "You know where she is?"
    "Yeah."
    "She still love you?"
    "I guess."
    "See? It ain't so bad. Why she move out?"
    "She's graduating. She doesn't want to live with her mom
anymore."
    He pets me. "You gonna miss her. I know that. She gonna
miss you too, sometime. But she a young woman now. She
need her independence." He kisses me. "You should be
proud of her."
    "I am."

"She a nice kid." He hands me my hamburger. "You need you some food, & a hot tub. Comeon." At the hot tubs, we make love first in the bed, then in the shower. As we relax in the tub, he rubs my shoulders. "Feelin better?"

"Um-hmm."

"See? You need some time, a little love. You be okay," he kisses me. "Am I right?"

"I still don't have my kid."

"No. But she sposed to grow up; you know that. You don't want some kid hoverin round the house watchin t.v. Am I right?"

"Umm."

"Women!" he mutters. "Come here." He carries me back to the bed. "We ain't leavin here til you smile."

Oakland • 1987 • Lorenzo

THE UNEMPLOYMENT RATE FOR YOUNG BLACK MALES IS 42%

When Lorenzo hears that one of my favorite students spent the night on a nearby roof with no blankets, he yells at him. "Why didn't you go to Alta's place?"

"He knows he can do that. Right, Zach?"

Zach shrugs.

"Don't you sleep outside in this weather," Lorenzo shakes his finger at him. "Not when you got a friend!"

After dropping Lorenzo at the bus stop, I return to find Zach, cold & shy, smoking a cigarette on the porch.

We pull out blankets & a futon. I tell him no drugs or violence, or he's back on the street. He nods silently.

After he goes to bed, I pray he'll get through this. My dear student, my brilliant young man, let our love make a difference.

Berkeley • 1988 • Lorenzo / Zach

114

When I turned 45, I didn't mention it to too many people. Lorenzo had a construction job out of town & couldn't take me out for our usual birthday dinner, but I came home to find a message on my machine. "Love you, Alta," it said, & then, "Happy birthday to you..." he sang the whole song on my little tape. I sat in the dark, playing it over & over again & crying. The town is full of middle-aged men chasing fertile young women & ignoring me & my kind, but my beautiful 24 year old is singing me happy birthday. Bless his heart.

He comes over when he gets back in town, & we celebrate. After we make love, I sigh happily, sniffing his chest. He smiles, "I'm *sposed* to smell good: I'm a *man!*"

Oakland • 1987 • Lorenzo